bad machine
Brooke Robinson

CURRENCY PRESS
The performing arts publisher

CAMP
BELL
TOWN
ARTS
CENTRE

CURRENT THEATRE SERIES

First published in 2022
by Currency Press Pty Ltd,
PO Box 2287, Strawberry Hills, NSW, 2012, Australia
enquiries@currency.com.au
www.currency.com.au
in association with Campbelltown Arts Centre.

Typeset by Brighton Gray for Currency Press.
Cover design by Ashley Murray.

Currency Press acknowledges the Traditional Owners of the Country on which
we live and work. We pay our respects to all Aboriginal and Torres Strait
Islander Elders, past and present.

A catalogue record for this
book is available from the
National Library of Australia

Contents

Bad Machine was first produced by Campbelltown Arts Centre at Casula Powerhouse Arts Centre, Casula, on 12 March, 2022, with the following cast:

EVE	Abbie-lee Lewis
MAY	Gail Knight
THEO	George Spartels
OLIVER	Rob Johnson

Director, Lily Balatincz
Composer/Sound Designer, Kirin J. Callinan and Robbie Balatincz
Lighting and Video Designer, Aron Murray
Set and Costume Designer, Emma White
Directing Mentor, Imara Savage
Stage Manager, Victoria Lewis
Assistant Stage Manager, Cindy Cavero
Creative Producer, Anthea Doropoulos

CHARACTERS

EVE, female, 35 years
MAY, female, 40 years
THEO, male, 60 years
OLIVER, male, 25 years

DOUBLING

Roles B and C should be assigned to the actors whose primary
character is not in the scene.

SCENE ONE. OLIVER

A party. OLIVER *shouts to be heard over the music.*

OLIVER: It's a grey area, that's what I'm saying.

B: Vigilantism?

OLIVER: I don't know why there's not more of it, actually.

B: Because we have the rule of law. Because we have a justice system. Because, most people, we believe in the social contract—

OLIVER: I don't know, if I was … maybe people should rise up a bit more.

B: 'Rise up'?

OLIVER: Stop complaining. Stop being disappointed by their systems and their governments and if they're being mistreated, actually do something about it.

B: 'People get the leaders they deserve' that sort of thing?

OLIVER: Maybe. Yeah.

B: What did the Syrians do to deserve al-Assad?

OLIVER: Nothing, I don't mean—

B: What did the Americans do to deserve Trump?

OLIVER: Are you really asking me that—

B: Okay, that one's too easy.

A brief pause. They both burst out laughing.

You're drinking the Limoncello aren't you?

OLIVER: It's just the right balance of bitter and sweet.

B: Sally from my torts class made it in her bathtub. It's lethal.

OLIVER: Manslaughter in NSW can you get a non-parole period of fifteen years. If I die of alcohol poisoning, Sally could be going away for a long time.

B: Too bad I'm not interested in criminal law otherwise I'd defend her.

OLIVER: What are you interested in?

B: I'm not sure yet.

OLIVER: No?

B: Still too early to tell.

OLIVER: It's almost nine-thirty. Twenty-five to ten, actually.

B: Maybe I'm interested in what's right in front of me.

OLIVER: I hope so.

A brief pause.

B: For a while I thought I was interested in intellectual property law. Patents and copyright and stuff. Scientists are fine, but there's too many wankers in the arts world. I mean, did you see that painting on the way in?

OLIVER: In this house?

B: The one that's just a dot. A tiny yellow dot on a huge white canvas. In the hallway.

OLIVER: Oh.

B: Have a look. It's hilarious. It has a sign underneath with the name of the artist and the gallery and the year and all that. So you know they paid bank for it.

OLIVER: Who?

B: The rich wankers who live here.

A very short beat.

Oh God.

OLIVER: It's fine.

B: I'm so sorry.

OLIVER: Don't worry, it's my parents' house. And they *are* wankers.

B: Are they here?

OLIVER: They're away this weekend. I'm twenty-five and I still have house parties when they're out of town. I'm living at home until I finish my Juris Doctor.

B: Where have they gone?

OLIVER: Down south. Near Berry.

B: They have a country house?

OLIVER: Yeah.

B: [*teasing*] A weekender? A property. 'An estate.'

OLIVER: I guess.

B: You're rich. I know why you're doing law, you're going to run for pre-selection for the liberal party aren't you?

OLIVER: *They're* rich. I have fifty dollars to my name until Tuesday.

B: I'm sorry. I'm teasing. This is a Sydney University postgraduate law party. Everybody's rich.

OLIVER: Except for you?

B: I'm on a scholarship. I'm a legal genius.

OLIVER: I have a scholarship too. Mine's called Centrelink Austudy.

B: Do you work as well? Or you just live off your trust fund?

OLIVER: I do some tutoring in the summer holidays but I have trouble keeping up with assignments during semester, as it is I'm only scraping in passes, the occasional credit.

B: That's okay.

OLIVER: I don't even *like* law. I'm only doing it because … my parents have their own firm. Mostly corporate clients, they expect me to work with them when I graduate. They pushed me to do law straight after school but I put them off. Backpacked around Europe until my grandmother's inheritance ran out. Now there's no escaping it, I'm destined to do contracts for the fine people of Macquarie Bank. I don't know why I'm telling you this.

B: So you don't like law. What *do* you like?

OLIVER: Maybe I'm interested in what's right in front of me.
[*Offering his hand to shake*] I'm Oliver.

SCENE TWO. EVE

EVE: I called an hour ago. I spoke to the manager about some tennis stuff?

B: That's me.

EVE: Right. Well, this. This here is brand new.

B: Looks like a robot.

EVE: It's a ball machine. Used, but only lightly. 2017 model. Good as new.

B: One of them robots that criss-crosses the carpet, vacuums your floor while you're out. This is lot bigger than they usually are.

EVE: It's for tennis.

B: Dogs are scared of them, moving around the house like they're alive. Cats attack them.

EVE: It's for tennis training, instead of playing with another person it will lob balls at you, one hundred, two hundred kilometres an hour. Toughens you up, lets you practice on your own. It's the training partner that never gets tired.

B: I can't sell this.

EVE: It'll slice, top spin, drop shot, make you run, practice your ground strokes.

B: No-one's going to buy this.

EVE: Do you know how many parents want their kid to be the next Serena Williams, Roger Federer? They'll pay anything.

B: Two hundred bucks.

EVE: It's worth four grand!

B: Best-selling items are slow cookers, golf clubs and air fryers. If you have any of those, bring 'em in.

EVE: Do you sell tennis rackets? I have—I can see you have squash rackets.

B: I can do you a deal if you wanna take both squash rackets.

EVE: I'm not buying, I—

B: Don't think I am either.

EVE: This one is used by Rafael Nadal.

B: I can give you twenty-five. Forty for the one with the green handle.

EVE: Now that. Ash Barty uses this brand.

B: Seventy dollars for both and I'll need to see some ID.

EVE: Nadal won two French opens with this racket. The strings have just been replaced.

B: You have a driver's licence?

EVE: Both are worth at least two-hundred and fifty new. The frames are in very good condition. You'll sell them by Easter, I promise you.

B: Slow cookers, air fryers, if you have any of them, bring 'em in.

EVE: Can we go back to the ball machine.

B: Those I can move.

EVE: As I say, it's worth four thousand dollars but—

B: The ring around your neck.

EVE: But I would be willing to accept as little as eight hundred dollars today only.

B: Three hundred for the ring.

EVE: Roger Federer did an ad for this ball machine in Japan.

B: I'll take the ring.

EVE: Digital billboards, screens all over Tokyo. Him hitting with this machine on a very blue court surrounded by mountains.

B: I'm about to change my mind.

EVE: The Japanese love robots. They believe machines are essentially soulful and good.

A pause.

You would, wouldn't you? Of course you would take the ring.

> EVE *slowly undoes a chain around her neck and considers the ring hanging from it. She hands it to* B.

Four hundred dollars.

B: Three hundred.

EVE: How do you know? How can you look at something and think you know what it's worth?

B: Cash. Sign here.

EVE: Will it go in the window?

B: Yeah.

EVE: Sell it to someone divine.

SCENE THREE. MAY

When B *speaks, they address the audience. When* C *and* MAY *speak, they whisper to each other.*

B: Welcome back everyone. Good lunch, yeah? I love the spinach and feta rolls these caterers do. Lovely. Alright, this afternoon we're going to cover the principles of—

MAY: What's this for anyway?

C: What?

MAY: The training. What is this about?

C: I don't know—

B: Key principles of Advanced Customer Aggression and Conflict. By the end of today, all of you, as managers, will be equipped with the necessary tools to go back to your contact centres and upskill your teams. It's my job to make you, as leaders, more robust and agile so that you can ensure the team behind you is resilient and confident. And who doesn't want that, yeah?

MAY: Is everyone here from human services?

C: I think so—

B: Alright. So. We're going to walk through some specific and experiential learning options to demonstrate de-escalation techniques that you and your frontline staff can use when dealing with challenging and aggressive customer situations.

MAY: What's a 'customer situation'?

C: Just a phone call—

B: When you go home tonight, you'll leave with the skills to identify an escalating customer situation and you'll know how to safely disengage.

MAY: Does that mean 'hang up' on them?

C: Yeah—

B: We'll also go through emergency response protocols and post-incident procedures. And, I'm sorry, I know not everyone is into it, but there will be some role-play. This is different to the usual, though, this is special. I promise, you'll love it.

C: Jesus.

MAY: Do you think I can fit through the bathroom window and make it to the car park?

C: You leave without me and I'll make your face into a 'customer situation'.

B: So. That is the plan for this afternoon. Sound good, yes? Alright. What else? Tea and toilet break is at three-fifteen so look forward to some shortbread biscuits with your Earl Grey. Before we get started on the scenarios, David from the Department is going to give you an exciting update on the roll-out of the Microsoft virtual assistants that Human Services will be pioneering next month. In a couple of years, I tell you, this AI is so good your team will all be virtual assistants and instead of training humans at Centrelink I'll be coaching computer programs. This is incredibly cutting edge. I'm honoured to be part of this, I really am. Take it away, David!

MAY: The phones are going to be answered by computer programs?

C: Apparently.

MAY: So then why are they bothering to train us in 'advanced aggression' now?

C: Something big is coming.

SCENE FOUR: THEO

THEO: Have some more beans.

B: Theo.

THEO: Come on my love, one more spoon.

B: *Theo.*

THEO: You prefer the bread. Do you want some more bread?

B: I want to go home.

A brief pause.

THEO: We are home.

B: I want to be there. When it's time. Soak in the air of our real home when I—

THEO: This is our home.

B: The farm is your favourite thing here and you've been wrenched from it.

THEO: The farm is still there.

B: You miss work.

THEO: What's to miss? The figs haven't changed in twenty years. My back aches. I stoop now. My hands are barely strong enough to rip the vines. This is better for me.

B: If we were at home, you could still be working. You would have more help. My sister.

THEO: We don't need your sister.

B: Cousins and the community and your nephews—

THEO: This is our community now.

B: You wouldn't be doing everything on your own.

THEO: If we were at home?

B: Caring for your wife like a nurse isn't natural.

THEO: Why nurse? Why not doctor? You don't think I'm smart enough to become a surgeon? I can still learn.

B: Slowly, each day a little worse and worse. Lumbered with me, every day the same.

THEO: You'll get well. It will take time. Now: beans.

B: You can't keep living like this.

THEO: I'm so grateful I can look after you. At home? You think we could live like this at home? That they have a 'carer's payment' in that country? *This* is our country. It's called a 'carer's payment' because they care. We live here now, and we are looked after.

B: What will you do when I'm gone?

THEO: Stop it now, have some more bread.

A brief pause.

B: I want my ashes to go in Sydney Harbour.

THEO: I want mine to go in the Sydney Cricket Ground!

B: The players will slip over your dust and lose the test match.

THEO: You'll poison the octopus.

B: I want a shark to eat me. A great white shark.

A brief pause.

THEO: Finish up and I'll help you into the bath.

B: I know you went to the fig farm yesterday.

THEO: First, your yellow tablet and then the big red one; I'll cut it in half.

B: You are not stuck at home caring for me. Know that.

THEO: I didn't go there to ask for my job back.

B: You can return to work the minute you tire of this.

THEO: Today is special, okay? A good test result.

B: I haven't beaten it Theo, all it is is more time.

THEO: Even one more day with you is a good result. So we are celebrating with honey and figs and cheese—that's why I went to the farm yesterday, to get figs. We are having dessert!

SCENE FIVE: EVE

EVE: Jana Novotna. Wimbledon. 1993. It's the championship final and we are in the third set. Novotna has won the second set six–one and is a point away from taking a five–one lead in the third. She is five points away from winning Wimbledon. The pinnacle of tennis, one of the world's greatest sporting contests. There's royalty in the crowd. Princess Diana is watching, Julia Roberts, Harrison Ford. Kevin Costner is there, remember him? It's 1993. Winning Wimbledon is what Jana Novotna has been training for her whole life. It's almost here. It's so close she can smell its armpits. And what does she do? She serves a double fault. She loses the match, the championship; she chokes. Imagine. The next day, all the newspaper headlines scream, all those cruel British tabloids run a headline, a variation on JANA NAVOTNA LOSES WIMBLEDON, THE PLAYER FROM CHOKE-O-SLOVAKIA.

(The Iron curtain is still up.)

That's what people think. Ask any tennis fan about the women's Wimbledon final 1993 and they will say that's the year Jana Navotna choked.

I suppose it's a glass half full/empty thing.

No. No it isn't. They're completely, totally wrong.

The 1993 women's Wimbledon final was the stage for one of the greatest tennis comebacks of all time. German player Steffi Graf won the first set, lost the second set in a thumping one–six and was thoroughly trailing in the third. Her opponent was five points away from winning the championship. She was down for the count. But what does Steffi Graf do? She hammers her forehand down the line, she serves up a few aces, some of the craftiest drop shots you've ever seen. And she *wins*. She comes back from imminent defeat and she turns things around.

The senior coach at the courts where I teach was playing a match on the weekend, just a hit and giggle thing. Did a serve volley and as she was jogging back to take an overhead smash, rolled her right ankle. It's sprained. Badly. Physio says she needs to keep off it for at least six weeks. It's week two of term now, so basically she's going to be out of action until after the school holidays. So guess who's going to be taking her students in the meantime? Guess who's going to be teaching four hours every afternoon, evening and all day Saturday?

Go on, guess.

It's me.

ME!

Thirty-five dollars an hour, twenty-eight hours a week and I've enough hours, I've MORE than enough hours and I'm off Newstart, done with Centrelink—I am gunna be rich.

It's not too late for me. I'm thirty-five if you're wondering, I know that probably comes as shock, I get carded at Liquorland all the time.

I am not crazy. I'm not deluded. I know it's too late for me to come back and win Wimbledon but there's still time, there's still plenty of time for me to scout, to find, to train the next Australian Wimbledon champion right here in Campbelltown.

I never choked. Don't think that of me.

I was down and now I'm coming back.

SCENE SIX. MAY

MAY: Okay chook, sit down for a second. Please. Will you sit down, please? Thank you.

B: What?

MAY: You've been asking me about pocket money.

B: Yes! Yes!

MAY: It's time for us to talk about it.

B: Yeeeessss!

MAY: We need to talk it through it first, alright? Listen.

B: Yeah, yeah, I'm listening, Mummy! How much??

MAY: Alright well to start you off, five dollars a week.

B: Aw, that's not fair!

MAY: Come on, wait, listen.

B: Jessie gets eight dollars and Mohammed gets ten dollars plus his grandfather gives him—

MAY: And next year, when you turn six, you will be able to earn six dollars a week. Okay? It will go up.

B: Not. Fair.

MAY: If you don't like it, it'll be nothing. Is that what you want? Eh?

B: No.

MAY: Alright. So. Five dollars a week, paid every Monday as long as you have done your chores for the week.

B: This is so bad.

MAY: Money has to be earned. We'll keep a record on the fridge. I want you to feed Scruffy in the afternoons, when you get home from school. And clean out her water bowl, okay? You can do that.

B: Yeah.

MAY: And on Sunday, after I've done the washing you can help me with folding and pairing up socks. Okay? You do that, and on Monday, every Monday, you'll get five dollars just for you.

B: Alright. Yeah.

MAY: Wait, I'm not finished yet. If you want to earn your pocket money you need to stay seated until I finish. Okay. Your pocket money will be made up of coins, okay? Silver and gold coins. You'll have three jars—jam jars from the recycling—you can decorate them how you want. One jar will be called SPEND and the money in that jar is for you to spend whenever, on whatever you want.

B: Like ice cream!

MAY: If you want to buy ice cream at school after football you can do that. The second jar is called SAVE. Now in that jar you put your coins, a few coins every week and eventually all those small coins will add up to a big amount of money and you'll be able to buy something you really want. Like that dinosaur set were looking at in Kmart the other week? Remember?

B: Stegosaurus Rex!

MAY: That cost thirty dollars and so you, getting five dollars each week, you can see that you would need to save, to wait for a while until you have enough money in your SAVE jar to be able to go back to Kmart and buy it.

B: How many five dollars until thirty?

MAY: There is a third jar called GIVE. Each week you need to put some coins, at least one coin in each of your three jars. You can't put all of your coins into one jar. You must spread them across. Make sense?

B: No! Why? That's not fair!

MAY: The one called GIVE is where you will be able to put some of your coins as a donation, to give to someone else who needs it more than you do.

B: I'm not putting ANYTHING in that jar!

MAY: Every week you have to put something in EACH jar. At least a couple of coins.

B: Five dollars! That's all I get! That's so bad! I'm not giving any of it away! No!

MAY: The coins that you collect in the GIVE jar, you can decide which charity you'd like to donate them to. You might like to donate them to a charity that gives children overseas in poorer countries pens and pencils for school.

B: No.

MAY: Or you could choose to give your GIVE money to the RSPCA. Remember that place we got Scruffy from? All the doggies that live there don't have homes yet and so they need people to give money to buy them food and toys to play with.

B: I'll put five cents in the GIVE jar. Five cents each week. That's it.

MAY: That would be very mean. I'd like you to think about that. I'd like you to think about being generous and what a nice person would do.

B: All my friends are already getting pocket money and getting lots more than I do, and they don't have to put any in some stupid jars.

MAY: Remember your cousin Greer?

B: She's in heaven.

MAY: That's right. *Now* she's in heaven, but before, she went to Disneyland with her mum and dad and she told you about it, remember?

B: I wanna go to Disneyland!

MAY: Disneyland costs a lot of money, and Greer and your aunt and uncle were able to go, were able to take Greer there before she went to heaven, because some nice people, some very generous people gave up some of their own money to pay for it. Money like your pocket money. Because Greer needed it more than them. Make sense? It's about giving some of what you have to someone else who needs it more. Not everything, not all you have. Just some, and you can spare it. You can.

You hope that you will never need money from other people but if you do, it's nice to know that others, nice people like you, will help to look after you. We all need to try to help each other, okay?

B: I miss Greer.

MAY: I know you do.

B: I'll do the GIVE jar.

MAY: Good boy. I'm proud of you.

B: Eww.

SCENE SEVEN. OLIVER

C: He has some very unrealistic expectations of the litigation process.

B: I told you that. Didn't I say that when I met the wife at their dinner party?

C: The client—

B: The first client or the second client?

C: The second. Somehow got the idea that it would be wrapped by June and the acquisition of the New Zealand parent company would be complete the day after.

B: No idea.

C: Then there's the son.

B: He works with them too?

C: Cokehead. Alcoholic. DUI charges up to his earlobes. Would have lost his licence if not for the counsel his parents hired last time.

B: They indulge him.

C: Pulled over again by police yesterday in Rose Bay. About to breath test him. While the officer's getting the machine ready he asks him: 'Have you had anything to drink tonight sir?' What does he do? He doesn't answer. Policeman tells him to blow into the machine and asks 'Have you maybe had one or two drinks tonight sir?' Still no answer. Cop is getting very impatient now, runs his plates and of course sees he's a frequent flyer. The officer tries one more time. Gets him to blow into the machine and he's WAY over the limit; the officer says now: 'Would you consider yourself a regular drinker sir? Maybe have four or five drinks each time you get behind the wheel?' Now he speaks, uses the steering wheel to pull himself up. He says: 'Four or five? I *spill* more than that each time I get behind the wheel.'

B: Tell me you won't make a recommendation.

C: I already I said I don't know any criminal lawyers. Only come to me when you're buying a company, selling a company, or throwing one under the bus.

OLIVER: Aren't you grateful you have me?

B: We have you the way you are because we never indulged you.

C: That's true.

B: You know the measure of hard work and you are prepared to do what it takes to get the result you want.

C: Speaking of which, how'd you go in your contracts exam last month?

OLIVER: Good, yeah.

C: Don't be shy.

B: Tell us, Ollie.

OLIVER: HD. High Distinction.

C: That's my boy!

B: Of course you did. You deserve it.

OLIVER: No, I, I got lucky with some of the questions.

B: You're too modest. You say that every time. A solicitor should not be modest.

C: They are still paying you that scholarship, aren't they? You have it for the full second year?

OLIVER: I, yeah, they're still paying me.

C: Not enough, I'm sure, but at least they're recognising your academic achievement. Your potential. They're lucky to have you, and they need to give you a scholarship to keep you.

B: We can't wait to have you at the firm.

C: Constitutional law this semester?

OLIVER: That's right, yeah.

C: Never my favourite area. Your mother was better at it.

B: You won't need my help, Ollie. I'll have forgotten it all anyway. Of course it's all almost entirely useless in a commercial setting.

C: But Bill at the firm is a bit of a constitutional nerd. Wishes he was a QC, really. If you want to speak to him about anything, we can set it up.

OLIVER: That'd be great, thanks Dad.

B: Can we toast, please?

OLIVER: No, Mum, really let's not.

B: I insist.

C: To our son the insufferably high academic achiever.

OLIVER: Oh God.

B: To the best legal student this side of Harvard. You could have gone to Harvard if you wanted to. Bet you would have got a scholarship there too.

C: Cheers!

OLIVER: Ah, okay, thanks cheers—

B: Cheers!

C: I love this beef. Chewy. Melty.

B: There's tiramisu in the fridge.

C: You're an angel. I bought a new bottle of pinot gris too. McClaren Vale 2017.

B: Oh don't forget, the cleaner is coming tomorrow morning so if you want to avoid any awkward dancing around her mop—be out of the house by nine.

C: Will do.

B: Oh Ollie, there's a letter came for you. Did you get it?

OLIVER: No?

B: On the hallway table.

OLIVER: I'll look, thanks.

SCENE EIGHT. EVE

EVE: Is it here? Tell me you haven't sold it.

B: Oh, you. Sold one of your tennis rackets yesterday.

EVE: The ring isn't in the window.

B: Gold number with the little sapphire. Sold it ten minutes ago. To a poxy little high schooler wanting something for Mother's Day.

EVE: Ten minutes ago? Do. No. Do you know who he was, did you get—

B: 'm teasing ya. It's here, I haven't done the window display yet. We don't keep valuables out overnight.

EVE: Please, can you get it.

He does.

B: This it?

EVE: Yes. Yes. Thank you!

B: You want to buy this back?

EVE: I have cash, the same notes you gave me and everything.

B: Change your mind? Can't part with the family jewels after all?

EVE: New job so, I'm alright for money now.

He takes the cash from her.

B: This is two hundred short.

EVE: It's three hundred. This is the exact three hundred dollars you paid me for the ring.

B: The ring is five hundred now, see the tag says so.

EVE: It was six days ago, not even a full week. Can't we just—

B: You wouldn't haggle in Big W, you can't haggle in here. It's five hundred dollars.

EVE: I'm not *buying* it, we're *reversing*, see? Reversing the *original* transaction that took place last week—

B: I'll put it back in the window then.

He turns his back to her and fiddles with the display.

EVE: I can bring in more tennis rackets. You said you sold one of mine already, I have half a dozen more at home, I …

Silence. B *still has his back to her.*

C *enters.*

C: Hey do you sell air fryers?

B: Up the back, along the wall.

C: Thanks.

C *exits.*

B: Air fryers and slow cookers …

B *turns back to face her.*

What I can do is take the three hundred cash from you today. You can take the ring home and pay off the two hundred dollar difference using one of our personal loans.

EVE: Oh yeah?

B: Easiest way to do it if the bank won't give you a credit card.

EVE: What's the interest rate?

B: Everything's in this document. You have time, you can read it.

EVE: I don't need to. I know what it says. By Friday that two hundred dollars becomes two hundred and fifty and next week it's up to two eighty and by the end of month I owe you three hundred and fifty then four hundred, five hundred by winter, of course I won't be using any heating, the electricity will probably be off, me getting further and further behind and eventually the interest I pay you is twice the value of the actual ring. You can write anything you want in your contract, it's just marks on a page to frighten people, crush people. Money isn't real.

B: I'm just trying to offer you a solution.

EVE: Ever noticed how the stuff you can't see is what causes human beings the most grief? God and love and money. What people will do for those things.

Keep the ring. Put it in the window. When I have five hundred dollars cash, I'll come back. If you sell it before, then … I hope that person is going to be okay.

SCENE NINE. THEO

B: Read it again.

THEO: Finish your meal. Don't think about it.

B: I feel sick, Theo.

THEO: You might feel better if you eat this, come on, some water too.

B: Read it to me again.

A pause.

THEO: 'We have reassessed your Carer Payment. You were paid more than you were entitled to and you need to pay the money back. The correct amount of your earnings was not taken into account in the payments made to you. This means you have been overpaid twenty-three thousand, four-hundred and seventy-five dollars and fifty-eight cents. Due Date: 19 May 2018.'

A pause.

B: Please, one more time.

THEO: It's a scam, I should throw it out. Like those people on the phone who say they're from the tax department and tell you to buy them Amazon vouchers. We don't have to worry. We don't fall for scams. It's going in the bin, when I take out the recycling. Do you want some black pepper?

B: You're sure it's a scam?

THEO: People fall for these, you know. Older people, those still improving their English. They should find them and they should be put in jail.

B: I'll ask Tia at the doctor's surgery if she got one.

THEO: Don't bother her, don't scare her, it's nonsense. How is your leg feeling this afternoon? We may need to change the dressing.

B: I've been keeping my weight off it. We can change it in the morning. Eat, relax.

A pause.

THEO: Tomorrow I'll be going out for a while so I've prepared you lunch and dinner, in the fridge alright? I know it's hard for you to lift the kettle but—

B: You'll be out at night?

THEO: I need to out in the morning. After breakfast, after your medication. I might be home late. Would you like a bath tonight or in the morning?

B: Where are you going?

THEO: I need to go into town to see, just some documents for tax and, the bank. You know I don't like to do it on the internet. Do you need anything from town?

B: Theo, your hand is, you're shaking.

THEO: I'll be going past the chemist, the supermarket of course. The post office too, do you need some stamps? Think about it and tell me in the morning. Anything you need.

B: This is about the letter.

THEO: They scam people. They should be put in jail.

B: I think it's real.

>   *A pause.*

THEO: I tried to call them this afternoon, during your nap? I was on hold for two hours. Nothing happening. Just music, the same notes over and over again. I hung up and tried while I was cooking? The same. I'll go into the Centrelink in town tomorrow. It's better to talk to their face.

B: Read it to me again.

THEO: Face to face they will know what to do. They'll say it's a scam and—

B: How much?

THEO: Twenty-three thousand, four-hundred and seventy-five dollars and fifty-eight cents.

B: You didn't look.

THEO: That's what it says, down the bottom.

B: Just then, you didn't look, you knew the number, you've memorised it.

THEO: [*quietly*] It's a scam.

>   *A beat.*

It would take a year to earn that much from the fig farm. But I can move to Sydney and—

B: Sydney?!

THEO: Like Max's son, remember? Move to Sydney for a few months and work, they have so many factories with vacancies, abattoirs, he did double shifts, seven days, I can earn twice as much as here, pay it off in a few months and it will go quickly, the time, I don't want to leave you.

B: Where would you live?

THEO: I spoke to Max today and he said his son—

B: Oh, Theo.

THEO: They have boarding houses close to the factories and abattoirs, his son is helping me, to see where I could go.

B: I can't go with you. All of my doctors and appointments here—

THEO: I know.

B: You shouldn't be made to do that kind of work at your age.

THEO: You shouldn't be made so sick at your age.

B: I shouldn't have ever drank alcohol. It could have been the powerlines I lived under before you, I shouldn't have lived in that house. The years I worked painting furniture, when they still put lead in paint, breathing it in, I should have got a different job, I …

> *A pause.*

THEO: Maybe you can come up for one day, maybe the doctors will say a weekend is alright and you can visit me and we can have a little holiday in Sydney! See the water and the bridge and the zoo! We can go on a boat and eat seafood and do whatever you want. Okay?

> THEO *is visibly shaking.* B *stills his hand.*

SCENE TEN. OLIVER

B: Are you sure?

OLIVER: Yeah I'm okay.

B: She can get you a flat white, anything.

OLIVER: I'm good, thanks.

B: I think you were in high school the last time I saw you.

OLIVER: I would have been, yeah.

B: Are you working in the family firm?

OLIVER: I will be soon. I did a business degree first, commerce, went travelling for a few years.

B: Nice, very nice.

OLIVER: I'm doing a Juris Doctor so…

B: Sydney University?

OLIVER: Yeah.

B: Best alumni network, brilliant.

OLIVER: They want me to, my parents—I'll be joining the firm once I graduate. Commercial law, most likely.

B: It's good to see you Oliver.

OLIVER: Thanks, you too.

B: What can I do for you today?

OLIVER: I inherited some money when my grandmother died.

B: Oh brilliant. I don't mean 'brilliant' that she—

OLIVER: It's fine, she died five years ago. I basically spent it all after university, after my undergraduate degree.

B: Travelling.

OLIVER: Exactly. I haven't really needed much cash since, I'm living at home while I finish this law degree and I tend to use my parents', the family money on day to day things.

B: Of course.

OLIVER: I know I have a pile of, some shares and other investments as part of the family trust? I don't know exactly. Some term deposits and I would like to—

B: You'd like to know where you stand. You're growing up, you want to take an interest and fully understand your financial position.

OLIVER: Yeah, that's—

B: Great, Oliver, I can help you with that.

OLIVER: Good.

B: I can go over most things with you today and I can also make an appointment for you to speak to one of our advisors in the private banking division.

OLIVER: The main thing is—I would like to know how much I have, what's available and what's locked away and I would like to liquidate some of what's there. Today.

B: By 'liquidate' you mean…

OLIVER: I'd like to have some of it, not much, at all, say twenty thousand in cash, in the bank account that's in my name.

B: Ah.

OLIVER: Is that, a problem…

B: No, no. It's your family's money, your investments, absolutely but … I don't want to disappoint you. I hope you understand it's not going to possible for me to turn any of your investments into cash *today*.

OLIVER: I thought some of it, at least some of it would be fairly liquid already? I mean, I don't want it coming from my parents' day to day bank account, but some of the other products in the family trust.

B: Are your parents or your sister joining us today?

OLIVER: Here? No, no.

B: It's only that the bank would require the signature of both your parents and your sister in order to make any significant change to your investment spread or to withdraw…

OLIVER: For my share? Even if it's nothing to do with their slice of the—

B: A signature would still be required, yes, perhaps we could—

OLIVER: Is there nothing that's only in my name?

B: Well the trust is, I'm afraid how your family's trust was established it does require the signature of *all* family members.

OLIVER: Okay.

B: I am sorry about the inconvenience but I'm sure you understand it's to protect your assets and to ensure—

OLIVER: Yeah, I. It's just that it's my parents', their wedding anniversary coming up, thirty years and—

B: Oh how lovely.

OLIVER: Yeah and I was hoping to buy them something nice, you know, they like art so I was thinking a fairly major piece from a gallery, one of those small galleries in Paddington. I thought I could take out some of my share of the money without them knowing. So I wouldn't be spoiling the surprise.

B: How thoughtful.

OLIVER: So any amount I can take out without requiring their signature would be helpful. I can buy an artwork that fits with that budget, whatever that turns out to be.

B: I am sorry Oliver. I can't make any changes to your investments without their signature.

OLIVER: Twenty thousand would be great.

A pause. They hold the stare.

B: Could you maybe—purchase the artwork with your sister or have your parents come in and sign and tell them the money is for something else? For your studies, perhaps?

OLIVER: I'll think of something.

SCENE ELEVEN. EVE

EVE: One of my players is late with their fees. He's a thirteen-year-old kid, a student of the head coach for over a year so I don't know if he's always late with payment or if he's trying it on because I'm new. It's awkward to bring up money with children. It's the reason I prefer to coach adults, you can look them straight in the eye and know, know if they're good for it or if they're living in some kind of fantasy land that something's gunna change for them real soon and they're going to be able pay, they're sure of it.

Back when I was first learning tennis, it was all cash, like everything, you fronted up to the court with your fold of notes, tucked it in the side pocket of the coach's racket bag or else you didn't get to play. Now the parents pay online and drop their kids off in the car park and you try to raise the issue on the court but they shrug their shoulders and say 'ask my mum'.

For the last three weeks I've been trying to catch this boy's mother before and after class. Tried calling her mobile a couple of times too but she doesn't answer. He never mentions a dad, I don't think there is a dad. Mum is probably broke but she's trying to be the best parent she can, desperate for her son to keep up his tennis lessons, the one hobby he has, though it's inevitable soon on Wednesday afternoons he'll be going straight home from school. Maybe he can keep up his game playing at home. That's how Monica Seles (nine time grand slam winner) and Andre Agassi (world number one for a hundred and one weeks) both trained—they grew up poor hitting a hairless ball against their house, bouncing it on a sad brick wall.

A pause, a sigh.

I need the money and I hate it but I have to ask his mum to pay me what she owes.

I've written it down. I can't catch her at the court or on the phone so I've written a letter outlining her debt and I'm putting it in the post this afternoon.

We have reassessed your Newstart Payment. You were paid more than you were entitled to and you need to pay the money back. The correct amount of your earnings was not taken into account in the payments made to you. This means you have been overpaid eleven thousand, three-hundred and forty-five dollars and ten cents. Due Date: 02 June 2018.

It's Tuesday. The boy will be coming for his usual lesson tomorrow. I won't ask him about money this week, I won't even look for his mum. I'll let him have this final class, I want it to be a good memory for him so I promise, I will, I'll make it extra fun.

SCENE TWELVE. MAY

MAY: I'M HOME. MUM? I'M HOME.
C: How's your day?
MAY: Yes, fine.
C: Really?
MAY: Work's just … a bit…
C: You look stressed.
MAY: How's the kid? He behave himself for you?
C: Yes, of course.
MAY: He's an angel now that he has something to lose. *Pocket money.*
C: You look tired.
MAY: You staying for dinner?
C: I can cook. You do look exhausted.
MAY: Tea? I'm putting the kettle on while I chop.
C: Did something happen today?
MAY: No, it's not … Nothing.

A short beat. MAY *relents.*

It's … new management, new programs…
C: They love you there.
MAY: I know it's … I've started looking. Applying for other jobs.
C: Still in the government?

MAY: Outside the public service. I want to try something in not for profits, maybe manage a call centre for a charity. Something like that.

C: Don't quit before you have something lined up.

MAY: I know.

C: Until you have it in writing!

MAY: Of course not, I … I applied for a job yesterday, I really hope I get. At Lifeline? You know the charity?

C: Oh yes.

MAY: It pays less, but …

C: May! *Less* money?

MAY: Mum, I've got to get out. Things are going to be really ugly at work soon and I want to flee before the ship sinks, you know?

C: There's always a period of adjustment with a new manager, you get along with everyone.

MAY: It isn't that. It's the new, the whole regime. Everything's automated now. Done by an algorithm.

C: So there's going to be job cuts?

MAY: I don't know.

C: Maybe you'll get a good redundancy.

MAY: I doubt it.

C: Maybe it's just a matter of holding on.

MAY: The government's insisting the department make savings of two-point-one billion. That's the target. The idea is that they're going to recover it from Centrelink customers. Issue debt notices.

C: Centrelink has been overpaying people? By two-point-one billion?!

MAY: Well, no. That's the thing, they haven't.

C: Then how are they going to force them to pay it back?

MAY: I don't know.

SCENE THIRTEEN. THEO/OLIVER

THEO *is on the phone to his wife.*   OLIVER *is in an inner city bar.*

THEO: The nurse should be
      coming tomorrow as well at
      eight o'clock. Tell me if she
      doesn't. I can't take my phone
      into the factory but I will have

a tea break around ten and I'll
check it then, okay? Leave
me a message, you need
something, anything, I'll call
you back around ten.

A brief pause.

B: 'Nother beer?
OLIVER: Yeah, yeah, I'll get it.
B: William Butler?
OLIVER: With the hot mum?
B: Doubt she's hot these days.
    Adman. Works for Saatchi in
    London. Went over straight
    after uni, never came back.
OLIVER: Right.

They drink.

The shifts are good, the
manager is nice. He's
from Thailand. Are you
remembering to take the white
pills with your breakfast?

A brief pause.

B: Terry Lee?
OLIVER: Oh yeah, with the ears?
B: Massive ears. Think tank in
    Canberra.
OLIVER: Yeah?
B: Government contracts, he's
    raking it in.
OLIVER: I bet.

Sydney is fine, it's nice.

A brief pause.

B: I don't see anyone much.
    Gareth sometimes.
OLIVER: How's he doing?

I am eating fruit.

A brief pause.

B: Still playing rugby. Seen a
few games together. He's
at a startup in Walsh Bay,
something to do with genetic
testing, I don't know.

OLIVER: And you're, you're still
at Goldman Sachs?

Your leg?

A brief pause.

B: Started six months ago. You
hear it from someone?

OLIVER: I thought you worked
there the last time we—

B: Nah I was at UBS then, lasted
two years. Haven't seen
anyone from school since I
started working there.

OLIVER: I think it was Facebook.
I saw it. LinkedIn.

B: You googling me? I like it.

You remember the oncologist
on Friday? I've booked a taxi
and you—

A brief pause.

OLIVER: You're, you're a day
trader there?

B: It's hectic but I'm looking
at pulling in half a mil this
year after commissions and
bonuses.

OLIVER: That's good.

B: Finally buy an apartment,
you know, Elizabeth Bay,
probably. Round there.

OLIVER: Great, yeah.

The meals are coming? The
deliveries are—

A brief pause.

Are you—taking on new clients?

B: 'Taking on new' what do you mean?

You tell me if something happens, if any of them—

A brief pause.

I don't really—my parents are into investing but I've never picked it up. Are you—do have retail clients, like individuals or …

B: Do you want some advice, mate?

Don't worry.

A brief pause.

OLIVER: Ah, okay.

B: Is that what this is about?

OLIVER: No, I wanted to catch up, I haven't seen you since …

I am eating.

A brief pause.

B: Travis's twenty-fourth—that was a shitshow.

OLIVER: It was, yeah.

I am eating right now.

A brief pause.

B: You want to start investing?

OLIVER: If I could, I mean I don't really know where to—

B: Okay. I can take you on. Side hustle.

Chicken with saffron rice and—

A brief pause. He looks at the
empty table before him.
A gravy sauce and roasted
tomatoes, lots of herbs—

   A brief pause.

Broccoli and bread and
cheese and there's tea too—

   A brief pause.

OLIVER: I don't have much to
   start off with, you know my
   money is tied up in the family
   trust and—
B: Start small. Aggressive.

Yes, just how I like it.

   A brief pause.

OLIVER: Is there a way, with yes,
   aggressive, short selling or—I
   have two grand and—
B: *Two* grand??

My belly is bursting. I have to
put it in the fridge to finish it
at lunch tomorrow. That's why
you can't hear me chewing.

   A brief pause.

OLIVER: To really smash it and
   double and triple it in a month
   you know like GameStop or
   bitcoin, before the crash I
   read that people were—
B: Challenge, bro.
OLIVER: Is it possible or—
B: *Two* grand? Fuck. Okay.

Oh yes, the men at the
boarding house are very nice.

   A brief pause.

I miss you.

A brief pause.

OLIVER: I'm a bit short on cash at the moment, you know, *liquid* assets while I finish my degree, so anything you could do to get me started would be—

B: Get me another beer and tomorrow, when the market opens, Oliver Wells, I will buy for you your first shares.

They high-five.

Continue drinking.

You are tired. You need to sleep.

A brief pause.

Don't worry about me. The men are calling me actually, knocking softly on my door to see if I'll join them for a game of cards or—

A brief pause.

So you can rest. Good night my love.

He ends the call. There is no knock at the door. He's hungry—there's nothing to eat.

He checks the time—it's only eight o'clock. He has nothing to do, no-one to talk to. He looks out of the window—there's no view. He paces his small room, but his body is exhausted. It's going to be a long night.

SCENE FOURTEEN: MAY

MAY: My passion is for people and results. I have a proven track record developing high performance teams. I champion the customer experience through understanding and connection at every interaction. I have extensive leadership experience, combining focus and innovation. I'm comfortable with ambiguity, thrive in changing environments and always see projects through and deliver tangible results. Where I really excel is my ability to build strong relationships and problem solve using the resources available to me. At Human Services I …

> *She forgets her place in the prepared speech. Laughs, smiles at the panel. Takes a breath. Rallies, tries again.*

At Human Services I …

> *A pause.*

I wasn't entirely honest. About what I said before.

> *A pause.*

I'm not good at interviews. Not that, I mean *that* part's true. *Shit.* Sorry. [*Re: swearing*] Oh God.

I don't thrive in changing environments. Well, it depends on the environment and the direction of change. What's going on there doesn't … align with my values. That's why I'm leaving. Because I can't. I won't do it. And this bit wasn't in the practice answers I've been rehearsing in the car for the past three days.

I'm sorry I've wasted your time.

> *A pause.*

Usually I'd need to give a month's notice but seeing as though the department is in a state of flux … yes I think I could start in two weeks.

SCENE FIFTEEN. THEO/OLIVER

THEO *is speaking into his phone.*

THEO: Hello, my love. You're
sleeping, that's good. I hope
this message won't wake
you. I'm having a tea break
at work, I'll call you again
tonight after my shift. I hope
you're feeling okay today.
Max said he mowed the lawn
and pruned the branches
overhanging the water tank.
I will bring him something
from Sydney, I don't know
what, maybe tell me what you
think he'd like.

　　I wanted to tell you,
properly, not in a message but
I can't wait—I booked my
bus ticket home. Two weeks
from today. I've earned
enough. For the debt, every
last cent. We did it, love. In
two weeks I'll be back to you
and we are free.

B: Beer?

OLIVER: No, thanks I'm okay.

B: It's Wednesday, practically the
　　weekend.

OLIVER: You go ahead I'm, I'm
　　good with a Coke.

B: So how's it goin?

OLIVER: Okay, yeah.

B: You're still at uni?

OLIVER: Few more weeks until the end of semester. Exams soon.

B: You'll kill it.

OLIVER: I don't know.

B: I went up to Byron last weekend. Have a client with a holiday house. Bro, *that* was a messy weekend. I'm still a bit sore to be honest. Saw Chris Hemsworth. Out on Saturday night with his missus. Now *she* is—

OLIVER: How is my investment?

B: Look. Bro. Stock-watching is never a good idea. This is long term, yeah? You've got to leave it there, let it breathe.

OLIVER: Long term? No, remember I told you I needed something fast—

B: I would recommend adding to your investment and considering it a medium to—

OLIVER: *Adding* to it? No, no, I told you that was all I had! You said you could double it.

B: Now wait a—

OLIVER: I need cash. You said you'd do something for me—

B: We're talking two grand. We dropped more than that on Dave's twenty-first. Chill.

OLIVER: What's happened to it?

B: That Coke isn't doing anything for you, have a beer.

OLIVER: How much are the shares worth?

Hello, my love. Calling again
to see if you are awake—it's
okay. When you get this,
I'll be back on my shift but
leave me a message or ring
the phone. So I know you're
alright? Thirteen days from
today. I'll see you soon.

B: Look. You are the proud
   owner of Bitecoin.
OLIVER: Bitcoin?
B: No. *Bitecoin*. The newest
   crypto. A very hot stock. I
   tried to short it. I did the best
   for you I could. These things
   aren't a sure thing. It went up,
   the price went up. You know
   with shorting—
OLIVER: I know what shorting is.
B: So. Look. I'd chalk this one
   up to experience and if you
   gave me fifty, a hundred
   grand then we could see about
   doing some serious—
OLIVER: It's gone? The whole
   two thousand dollars is
   gone?!
B: It was worth a punt. Bitecoin
   is going to be the hot new—
OLIVER: SHIT!
B: You got beer on my suit. Bro,
   my suit is worth five times the
   cash you just lost on Bitecoin.
OLIVER: *You* lost it. Not me. I
   ASKED you what you could
   do and you …
B: What's going on with you?

THEO *is listening to his voicemail.*

B: Theo, mate, it's Max from next door. Layla's fine, she's right here next to me. I just popped in 'cause she asked me to read a letter that came in the mail for ya, with the centrelink logo. Actually the AFP logo is on here too.

Listen. If you're in any strife, if there's anything I can do …

Alright, here goes.

'We have reassessed your Carer Payment. You were paid more than you were entitled to and you need to pay the money back. The correct amount of your earnings was not taken into account in the payments made to you. This means you have been overpaid thirty thousand, eight-hundred and seventy-four dollars and fifty-eight cents. Due Date: 21 August 2018.'

I'm gunna put Layla on.

A brief pause.

OLIVER: I owe the, the government eight grand.

B: [*laughing*] *Eight* grand? What, you got audited by the ATO?

OLIVER: I'm doing this degree, I can barely cope with the assignments, I get a few hours work here and there tutoring, that two grand was the only money I had in my name. I can't touch the family trust. My parents own everything. They don't know about, I don't want to have to ask them for, they're forcing me to work in the firm and I gave you every bloody cent I have and you pissed it away like it's nothing to you.

B: It *is* nothing to me. It's two grand.

No.

She's a bit upset at the moment to talk, she says she'll call you back later.

Mate, she showed me the previous letter. You owed them twenty-three thousand now it's thirty thousand. That can't be right. Don't stress, yeah, it must be a mistake. I just wanted to read it out to you.

Okay. I'll go now, Layla's okay.

OLIVER *glasses his friend with his schooner glass. The room freezes.* OLIVER *realises his friend's blood is covering his hands, hot and sticky and deep red and spreading up to his elbow.*

OLIVER: No, no, no, no. Oh shit. Are you. No, no, no.

SCENE SIXTEEN. EVE

EVE *is practicing her ball toss. She is doing drills at the back of the court, running along the baseline. She's pleased with her performance. She keeps an eye on a stopwatch—maybe she's hitting a recent personal best.*

Her mobile phone rings. The tone pierces the air like an alarm. She stops dead. Frozen. She knows who this is. Fight or flight.

SCENE SEVENTEEN. THEO

THEO: I need to use the internet.

B: Good morning. Are you an existing member?

THEO: Can I use these machines?

B: Do you have a valid library card?

THEO: No, I'm not—I don't live here, normally. I want to—

B: Not to worry. We'll get you signed up. I'll get you to fill out this form and let me know when you're finished.

> *A long pause.*

THEO: Hello? Can you help me?

B: How are you going there, all done?

THEO: I don't understand what this is asking me.

B: What do you have in the way of proof of address?

THEO: I don't live here, normally, not in Sydney, I just want to—

B: I'm sorry sir, I don't quite understand what you mean.

THEO: Centrelink. I need to research Centrelink payments, how they are calculated.

B: This isn't Centrelink, sir, this is a library.

THEO: I know this is a library!

B: Centrelink is—I think the closest branch is probably Surry Hills maybe?

> [*To off*] Vicki? Do they still have a Centrelink in Surry Hills?

THEO: I need to use the internet, please. Get onto the Centrelink website.

B: How are you going with that form?

THEO: I don't understand the form!

B: What about proof of address?

THEO: I live in a regional area, I don't drive, I don't have a licence, I didn't bring anything with me like bills or, I didn't think I'd need it.

B: How are you going with that form?

THEO: I just need to use the internet, please!

B: What about proof of address?

THEO: The Centrelink website.

B: This isn't Centrelink, sir, this is a library.

THEO: I know this is a library!

B: Centrelink is—I think the closest branch is probably Surry Hills maybe? [*To off*] Vicki? Do they still have a Centrelink in Surry Hills?

THEO: Google. I need to get onto Google.

B: How are you going with that form?

THEO: I just need to use the internet, please!

B: What about proof of address?

THEO: The Centrelink website.

B: This isn't Centrelink, sir, this is a library.

THEO: I know this is a library!

B: Centrelink is—I think the closest branch is probably Surry Hills maybe? [*To off*] Vicki? Do they still have a Centrelink in Surry Hills?

THEO: Okay. Okay. The Greyhound bus website. I need to change my ticket.

B: This isn't Greyhound, sir, this is a library.

THEO: I know this is a library!

B: Greyhound busses—I think the closest stop is probably Surry Hills maybe?
[*To off*] Vicki? Do they still have a Greyhound bus office in Surry Hills?

THEO: Stop. Stop it. Please just STOPPPP!!

SCENE EIGHTEEN. MAY

A Lifeline contact centre.

MAY: Ready?

C: I'm free.

MAY: Line four has been on hold for fifteen minutes. Let's go.

> *We see* MAY*'s colleague* C *take the call. We don't hear what* C *is saying but we see that they are speaking and listening to a caller, counselling someone over the phone.* MAY *watches and listens.*

C *continues the call.* MAY *whispers to another colleague in the room,* B. *It's a live training session.*

[*To* B, *re:* C] Observe how he's letting the caller set the direction of the conversation. His tone of voice.

B *nods they understand, they're listening.*

Are you hearing this?

B: They're talking about their tax? They missed a payment and—

MAY: No. I worked at Human Services. Supervising Centrelink calls before I came to Lifeline.

A brief pause. C *continues to speak and listen to the caller.* B *and* MAY *listen on.*

These debts—I know what this is about. They're not real. There's an algorithm that's falsely calculating hundred of thousands of debts for people who've received Centrelink payments. They don't owe anything.

B: [*re:* C] Is he going to refer them to financial counselling services?

MAY: That voice—where are they calling from?

B: Ah … it says New South Wales. Sydney.

MAY: Twenty years of supervising contact centres, I'm not good with names and faces but I remember a voice.

B: Do we ever refer people to Human Services? Put them in touch with Centrelink to help with their issue?

MAY: Centrelink *is* their issue.

MAY *finds a pen and writes 'LET ME SPEAK TO THEM' on a piece of paper.*

[*To* B] I wouldn't normally—don't record this in your training notes.

MAY *holds the message up to* C *who reads it whilst still on the phone.*

C: Sorry. They're gone.

SCENE NINETEEN. OLIVER

OLIVER: Mum. I thought you'd be at work.

B: I was in the middle of a partner meeting.

OLIVER: Where's Dad?

B: Not answering his phone. Probably still in the tribunal.

OLIVER: Is everything okay?

B: [*faux delight*] Whatever do you mean?

OLIVER: You, you don't normally drink in the morning.

B: Want some brandy, Oliver?

OLIVER: I just had breakfast.

B: Oh go on, what's the harm.

OLIVER: Mum, you're scaring me.

B: I'm scaring you. *I'm* scaring *you.*

OLIVER: What's going on?

B: I better not put this bottle down. You might smash it. Stab me in the eye with the shards.

OLIVER: You're still angry about the police … he won't press charges. He's my—*was* my mate.

B: You have something to tell me, Oliver?

OLIVER: I swear, I've never done anything like that before, I was stressed about uni, my exams and—

B: And your welfare fraud.

    A beat.

OLIVER: You. You saw …

B: They're threatening you with jail, Oliver. Centrelink!!

OLIVER: I've been getting Austudy. I'm entitled to it.

B: You're not on a scholarship, are you?

OLIVER: I'm a postgraduate student, over twenty-five, I don't have any assets or proper income, so I can get it. I didn't do anything wrong.

B: THEN WHY ARE YOU GETTING THESE LETTERS?

OLIVER: I don't know. Mum, you're scaring me.

B: [*reading the letter she found in a sing-song voice*] 'You have been overpaid. That means you have to pay it back. Spelt out to you like you're a retard. Because they assume you are. Because that's who gets these payments.

OLIVER: I can pay it back. It's only eight thousand dollars. I was thinking I could start at the firm, go part time at uni and work with you and Dad, I can earn enough to pay it back by, within a few months—

B: I already rang them. It's settled.

OLIVER: I'm sorry Mum. I'll pay you back, I …

B: You think I care about eight thousand dollars? The cleaner found your debt letters. Dusting the spare room she saw them poking out between the books. She read them. The woman who scrubs our toilets, who pulls our hairs out of the drain knows that this family receives welfare.

You should have seen the glint in her eye.

A very brief pause.

I paid her until the end of the month, asked her to leave before she'd done the kitchen.

OLIVER: It's not her fault, Mum, I shouldn't have—

B: So you can do it. She left her gloves under the sink.

SCENE TWENTY. MAY/EVE

MAY: [*on the phone*] Mum? It's me. [*A brief pause*] Fine, yeah. I'm about to order pizza—I don't feel like cooking tonight. Listen. Why I'm calling—are you going to church on Sunday? [*A brief pause*] I thought I might come, bring your grandson. [*A brief pause*] Yes, I'm serious! [*Laughing, a brief pause*] It can't hurt. To come, once. [*A brief pause*] Because maybe you're right about it. [*A brief pause*] Everything, all of this.

EVE: [*to herself, as a mantra. Maybe she's saying it in the mirror? Each time she says it, it becomes more desperate, less convincing, loses power*] Jana Novotna. Wimbledon. 1993. Championship final. Match point. Don't choke. I won't choke … Jana Novotna. Wimbledon. 1993. Championship final. Match point. Don't choke. I won't choke … Jana Novotna. Wimbledon. 1993. Championship final. Match point. Don't choke. I won't choke … Jana Novotna. Wimbledon. 1993. Championsh—

Meanwhile, THEO *is walking along the side of a dusty road. He's been walking for quite some time. He stops, looks in front of him, looks behind—he realises that he's lost. He presses on, resumes walking forward. He stops again, it's no use. He drops down into the dirt. It's a heavy fall—he'll struggle to get up on his own.*

Meanwhile, OLIVER *is cleaning his house as his mother instructed. He fetches the gloves from underneath the sink. He*

takes out bottles of cleaning fluid and starts scrubbing the floor.
He stops, looks at the bottles—bleach, etc. All poisons. The:
'CAUTION MAY CAUSE DEATH' has caught his eye. He slowly
takes off his gloves and starts reading the 'WARNING!' label.

SCENE TWENTY-ONE

EVE *is on a tennis court.* THEO, MAY *and* OLIVER *are all speaking on their phones. They are in different spaces.*

EVE: He came again yesterday. I was teaching two late private lessons, the second finished at eight o'clock. It was pitch dark by the time I collected all the balls. I took my shoes off like I always do, walked around on the floodlit spiky artificial grass. His was the only car in the parking lot.

OLIVER: Mum? Dad? I guess it'll be after six by the time you get this. You don't need to call me back.

THEO: Layla? Are you there? Have you forgotten to charge the phone? Please call me.

EVE: I knew who he was. He's come to my house a few times, smashed his knuckles against the window and left his angry letters piled on my mat. Whenever I hear footsteps approach my front door, I hide under the bed.

So now he comes to the courts.

MAY: [*automated voice*] *You have reached the National Suicide Prevention Lifeline. If you are in emotional distress or suicidal crisis or are concerned about someone who might be, we're here to help. Please remain on the line while we direct your call to the nearest crisis centre in our network.*

OLIVER: I don't want to finish my degree. I don't want to be a lawyer.

THEO: Max? Oh thank God. I can't get through to Layla.

EVE: Last night he stood there in the shadows until my last student left and it was dark and empty, even the moon was tucked away. He crawled up to the baseline, eyes fixed on me and I snapped the lock on the gate. 'Two more days to pay' he barked into my face. He gripped the wire fence and rattled. 'Then you'll be going to jail.'

THEO: The key is under the lemongrass plant—can you. Check.

MAY: Can I start with your name, please?

OLIVER: I told you I had a scholarship but I'm barely passing each semester and I can't. I can't do it anymore.

MAY: Hi, Oliver.

EVE: Tennis courts are always surrounded by tall fences. They're a cage. You need to fight your way out.

'I can pay,' I said. 'I'm trying to—I'm going to pay. Please,' I said. 'I need a few more days.' He shook the gate and I cowered behind the net until he left.

I can pay.

OLIVER: I'm not coming home today.

THEO: Go in. Yes, yes, the first door on the right.

MAY: How did that make you feel?

EVE: I fully intend to pay this debt. I need to sell this ball machine and then I'll have the money. I'm going to try a new Cash Convertors tomorrow, I just need to get the right person, someone who understands, who knows the game, who'll look and know what it's worth. Because it is a top-of-the-line machine.

OLIVER: Don't worry about me.

THEO: She's asleep. Those pills she takes.

MAY: I'm here for you, Oliver.

OLIVER: Please just—don't fire the cleaner.

EVE: The thing about tennis is it's an individual sport but you're always reliant on other people. You can serve on your own, work on your fitness, practice your footwork but there's two sides to a court, you'll always need another person to play.

THEO: Shake her, Max. Nudge her to wake her up.

MAY: Stay on the line, Oliver.

EVE: Well, *you did*. Until someone invented the ball machine. A technological marvel and now you can train, can hit all day, every day, without ever needing another human.

And the machine is tough to play. It never makes mistakes. It doesn't get tired, or emotional, it's infallible, it will wear you down.

OLIVER: I'm sorry that I embarrass you.

THEO: You need to shake her awake, those pills are strong.

EVE: That's the best thing about it. You want to get good at tennis? Try beating a ball machine that does high-speed internal, vertical, triple oscillation, the spin it produces is incredible, you won't defeat it.

MAY: Oliver, I have your location.

THEO: She's always cold, it's her circulation. Max?

OLIVER: I'm about to get the beep, the machine will cut me off, so …

EVE: It's worth four thousand dollars but I'll take three. Two and a half. It's eight o'clock, my last student has left. He's here again, in the parking lot. He hasn't approached the court tonight, I think he's waiting for me to leave, to follow me home.

MAY: I'm not going anywhere. Talk to me, Oliver.

THEO: Max? No, Max. You're not doing it right.

OLIVER: I think I'm gone.

EVE: I lock the gate. Lock myself in. The floodlights stay on all night, I'm safe here, he can't get to me. I sit on the synthetic grass and throw balls against the fence. I see his face through the gaps.

MAY: I'm contacting emergency services. They'll be with you in approximately five minutes. Please Oliver, stay on the line.

EVE: A tennis court is a cage you have to fight your way out.

MAY: My name is May.

THEO: SHAKE HER!

OLIVER: Gone.

MAY: Talk to me. Oliver.

   OLIVER.

   Beat.

NOOOOO!

   A tennis ball rolls across the stage.

THE END

bad machine

Brooke Robinson

12–19 March 2022

Playwright
Brooke Robinson

Director
Lily Balatincz

Cast
**Rob Johnson, Gail Knight,
Abbie-lee Lewis, George Spartels**

Composers/Sound Designers
Kirin J Callinan and Robbie Balatincz

Lighting and Video Design
Aron Murray

Set/Costume Designer
Emma White

Directing Mentor
Imara Savage

Stage Manager
Victoria Lewis

Assistant Stage Manager
Cindy Cavero

Creative Producer
Anthea Doropoulos

Campbelltown Arts Centre

Located on the edge of Sydney, Campbelltown Arts Centre (C-A-C) is in a unique position to forge collaborative exchanges between artists, disciplines and communities through the creation of new curatorial situations and challenging streams of practice.

Using the edge as a starting point, C-A-C creates a secure platform for communities and artists to take risks, challenge perceptions, confront issues and raise questions through the commissioning of new works. These new works invite collaboration, partnership, local, national and international dialogue, the juxtaposition of new and traditional techniques and cross-disciplinary approaches. Contemporary artists are at the forefront of C-A-C's programming and through consultation with communities, we deliver a program that profiles contemporary visual arts, performance, dance, music, live art and emergent practices.

Located on Dharawal land, C-A-C is proudly owned by the people of Campbelltown. A cultural facility of Campbelltown City Council and assisted by the NSW Government through Create NSW, Campbelltown Arts Centre receives support from the Crown Resorts Foundation, the Packer Family Foundation and the Neilson Foundation.

Brooke Robinson
Playwright

Brooke Robinson is an emerging playwright from Campbelltown in Sydney's South-West. She is a graduate of the Australian Theatre for Young People's Fresh Ink writers ensemble, Stephen Jeffreys' invitational writers group at the Royal Academy of Dramatic Art (London), The Criterion Theatre's invitational West End writers group in London and City, University of London where she completed a double MA in Playwriting and Screenwriting.

She was one of six artists to be commissioned for *Imagine 2037*, the imaginary theatre festival for the British Council's 20th Anniversary Edinburgh Festival Showcase and has had new scripts read and presented at other UK theatres including London's Drama Studio, Bunker Theatre, White Bear Theatre and The Traverse Theatre in Edinburgh. *Oysters*, a short play on the British role in the international arms trade, was commissioned by London's Old Vic theatre for a special event in December 2019. She is currently under commission to Sydney's Griffin Theatre after winning the 2020 Lysicrates Prize for a new comic play on ethics and science.

Brooke Robinson's plays include *Good Cook. Friendly. Clean* (Griffin Theatre Company), *Dangerous Lenses* (Theatre 505, Sydney; The Sub Station, Melbourne and Vault Festival, London, UK), *Animal/People* (Tamarama Rock Surfers) and *The Telescope* (Red Line Productions for the Old Fitzroy Theatre).

Lily Balatincz
Director

Lily Balatincz is a performing artist, dramaturg, producer and emerging director who was born and raised on Darug Country in Western Sydney. She is a graduate of the NYU Tisch School of the Arts Graduate Acting MFA program and UNSW.

Her directing credits include *From Nowhere to Now Here* (Tempo Rubato, Melbourne), *She Bit Her Tongue* by Caryl Churchill (Studio Tisch, New York) and *GFM*, co-directed with Dina Shihabi (Freeplay Festival, New York).

As a performer, she has worked on the development and premiere of new theatre works *The Eggs* by Adam Rapp (NYC), *Meantime* by Alexandra Gersten-Vassilaros (NYC), *Stop the Virgens* by Karen O (NYC and Sydney), *Weak Trembles* by Hal Corley (NYC) and *I Ragazzi* by David Goldsmith (NYC).

For her performance work, she has been the recipient of the 2017 Helen Hayes Award for Outstanding Lead Actress in a Play in Washington DC, the Dame Joan Sutherland Award and the Ron Van Lieu Yale School of Drama Scholarship. Balatincz was the 2020 Japan Foundation delegate for Australia for the Tokyo Performing Arts Meeting (TPAM) in Yokohama. She is currently a peer reviewer for Australia Council for the Arts and the American Australian Association.

Rob Johnson
Actor (Oliver)

Rob Johnson is an actor, comedian and writer. Some of his recent credits include *The Boomkak Panto* (Belvoir), *Calamity Jane* (Belvoir/One Eyed Man), *The Torrents* (STC/Black Swan), *Spamalot* (One Eyed Man), and *Rosehaven* (Guesswork/ABC). For the stage he has written *The Recidivists* (Red Line Productions) and *Fat On Purpose* (Giant Dwarf).

For his performance as Francis Fryer in the national tour of *Calamity Jane,* Johnson was nominated for the Green Room Award, Sydney Theatre Award and Glug Award for Best Supporting Actor in a Musical. He is a two-time NSW Theatresports Champion, and was a national finalist for the Equity/Second City Comedy Scholarship in 2020.

Rob Johnson's short stories have been published by *Overland, Aniko Press, Underground* and *Literatus,* and his non-fiction by *Audrey Journal* and *Switched On Media.* He was the winner of the 2020 Albury City Short Story Award, the 2018 Hal Porter Short Story Prize and the 2012 Best of Times Short Story Competition, and was shortlisted for the 2015 John Marsden and Hachette Australia Prize for Young Writers.

Gail Knight
Actor (May)

Now a seasoned performer in the commercial world of television guest roles, TV commercials and voice overs, Knights's first foray into her three-decades-long, full-time performance career, kicked-off with stage.

Beginning in 1989 at the much lauded Kent Street Theatre in Sydney, Gail's first role was in *Steel Magnolias*, where the character of Annelle allowed her to explore a flair for character acting and accents, while also unearthing a hidden talent for hairdressing.

Gail Knight continued to perform on various independent stages in Sydney and then Melbourne, from tap dancing in *Dinkum Assorted* to the deliciously farcical *Absurd Person Singular*, and the beautiful Irish play *Dancing at Lughnasa* for Heidelberg Theatre Company.

Since joining RMK Management in 2002, Knight has staked her place as a natural performer who constantly seeks to blend live performances with a successful voice over career. Recent performances include portraying a wife of an injured worker at the Hanson Safety Conference and a day-long improv performance to healthcare professionals, depicting three women living with gynaecological cancer.

Abbie-lee Lewis
Actor (Eve)

Abbie-lee Lewis is a graduate of the Aboriginal Theatre Course and the Acting Diploma Course at the Western Australian Academy of Performing Arts (WAAPA). Since moving to Sydney, Lewis has worked with Bell Shakespeare touring their educational program, The Players. The Players gave Lewis a chance to hone her classical acting skills as well as work with directors like James Evans, Janine Watsons and Scott Witt. Whilst working on the educational main stage production *A Midsummer Night's Dream* (2016) as a part of the The Players program, Lewis had the opportunity to play Puck. She worked alongside fight director and movement coach Nigel Poulton during this process and it was here she found a passion for physical theatre.

Abbie-lee Lewis was asked to return in 2017 to perform in the educational main stage production of *Macbeth*, where she again worked with James Evans and Scott Witt. More recently, she has appeared in *Our Town* (2019) for Black Swan Theatre Company and *The Bleeding Tree* (2021) for Perth's The Blue Room Theatre. In early 2017 she also worked on the original new work by Seanna Van Helten, *Fallen,* directed by Penny Harpham and produced by Sport for Jove.

George Spartels
Actor (Theo)

George Spartels is a familiar face to Australian audiences of all ages, thanks to his many appearances over the years in ABC's *Play School* and as Benito Alessi on *Neighbours*. Spartels has worked across the board in film, television and theatre for over 30 years. On stage, Spartels has worked with most of the major state theatre companies.

Theatrical highlights include: *Godspell* (original Melbourne production), *The Last Confession,* alongside David Suchet (London, Toronto, LA, Australian tour), *Hamlet* (STC), *Chicago* (STC), *Signal Driver* (QT), *Romeo & Juliet* (State Theatre Company SA), *The Levine Comedy* (MTC), Mike Leigh's *Greek Tragedy* (Sydney, Edinburgh and London seasons), *Losing Louis* (Ensemble Theatre), and *The Spook* for Belvoir Street Theatre.

George Spartels has also appeared in *Stool Pigeon*, a one-man show for the Sydney Festival. Television appearances include: *Packed to the Rafters, All Saints, Homicide, Cop Shop, GP, Fallen Angels, Rafferty's Rules, The Great Bookie Robbery, The Sullivans* and *Sweet and Sour*. His film roles include *Blame it on Burumba, Seeing Red, Mad Max III—Beyond Thunderdome, Out of it* and *Kick*.

Kirin J Callinan
Composer/Sound Designer

Kirin J. Callinan is a singer, songwriter and guitarist. He is a founding member of Mercy Arms, and has played and collaborated with the likes of the Night Game, Jack Ladder and the Dreamlanders, Genesis Owusu, Mark Ronson, Alex Cameron and Connan Mockasin. He's known for his exuberant public persona and diverse musical output.

Callinan launched his solo career in 2009 with the release of *Am I a Woman, Yet?* His *Way II War* music video won the 2012 J Award for Australian Video of the Year. Callinan's third solo record *Bravado* (2017) reached number five on the ARIA Hitseekers Album Charts, and the video for single *S.A.D.* was nominated for Best Video at the 2017 ARIA Awards.

Robbie Balatincz
Composer/Sound Designer

Robbie Balatincz is a sound designer and musician hailing from Western Sydney. He is a graduate of the Bachelor of Music program at Western Sydney University.

Working across film, TV, commercial and music production, recent screen credits include *After She Died* (dir. Jack Dignan), *Sink* (dir. Cloudy Rhodes), *Twig* (dir. Adrian Nugent) and *Setaceous* (dir. Tel Benjamin).

As a musician, Balatincz has been a member of bands The Griswolds, Megastick Fanfare and Cassette Kids (touring member) and has toured Australia, the US, the UK and Europe.

Aron Murray
Lighting and Video Design

Aron Murray is an emerging designer with a passion for the visual. His work incorporates projection, live camera and augmented reality with the goal of creating unique, cutting edge ideas and effects for live performance.

Receiving his formal performing arts training from the National Institute of Dramatic Art (NIDA), Murray holds a Master of Fine Art in Design for Performance as well as a Bachelor of Fine Art in Technical Theatre and Stage Management.

Aron Murray enjoys the unique creative opportunities offered in independent theatre and has worked on productions including *Rudy and Cuthbert Too* (KXT Theatre, 2019), *Degenerate Art* (Old Fitz, 2018), *Halftime* (The Hayes, 2021) and *This Genuine Moment* (La Mama, 2021).

Emma White
Set/Costume Designer

Emma White is a set and costume designer for stage and screen. White is a graduate of NIDA's MFA Design course and has a BFA in Sculpture from UNSW Art and Design. In 2019, White was nominated for an APDG Award for Best Emerging Designer for Live Performance and was selected for APDG's Mentor program. Since graduating, White has worked regularly as a design assistant to Elizabeth Gadsby alongside working in the costume department at Belvoir.

Emma White's theatre credits as Set and Costume Designer include: for Griffin Theatre, *Green Park*; for Belvoir 25A, *Kasama Kita*; for Bondi Feast, *The Knife*; for The Blue Room Theatre/Sotto, *You've Got Mail*; for Milk Crate Theatre, *Natural Order*; for National Theatre of Parramatta/Sydney Festival, *Boom*; for NIDA, *Stay Happy Keep Smiling* and *Venus in Fur*; for the Old 505, *Homesick*; for the Old 505/Sotto, *Safe;* for Q Theatre, *Daisy Moon Was Born This Way*; for Red Line Productions at the Old Fitz, *Chorus*. Her credits as Associate Designer include: for Hayes Theatre Co., *American Psycho*; for Sport for Jove, *A Misdummer Night's Dream* and *The Tempest*. As Assistant Designer credits include: for National Theatre (UK), *Nine Night;* for Shakespeare's Globe, *Richard II;* and for Sydney Theatre Company, *Lord of the Flies*.

Imara Savage
Directing Mentor

Imara Savage is a theatre and opera director. She has directed award-winning productions for Sydney Theatre Company, Belvoir Theatre, State Theatre Company of South Australia and Sydney Chamber Opera. Some of her award-winning productions include *Saint Joan, Mr Burns, Top Girls, Machinal, The Brother's Size, Hayfever, After Dinner, Fool for Love, Woyzeck, In the Penal Colony, Owen Wingrave* and the *Passion of Simone*. She has presented work at the Melbourne, Adelaide and Sydney festivals, and has also worked as a dramaturg with the Australian Ballet.

Imrama Savage is a graduate of NIDA in Directing and the NIDA Playwriting Studio and holds a BA in Communications and International Studies from the University of Technology Sydney.

Victoria Lewis
Stage Manager

Victoria Lewis is a stage manager, choreographer, director and performer. Lewis was the stage manager for New Theatre's production of *The Lovely Bones* (dir. Deborah Mullhall), *Pygmailon* (dir. Deborah Mullhall), *The Removalists* (dir. Johann Walraven) and assistant stage manager for *Lieutenant of Inishmore* (dir. Deborah Mullhall). Lewis has choreographed for New Theatre's production of *The Grapes Of Wrath* (dir. Louise Fisher), Penrith Musical Comedy Company's production of *Big: The Musical* and DZ Deathrays's music video *Like People* (dir. Guss Mallmann). *Like People* was nominated for Triple J's J Award for Best Music Video of the Year 2018.

Victoria Lewis was assistant director for New Theatre's production of *Neighbourhood Watch* (dir. Louise Fisher). She has also performed in theatre shows such as *How To Make A Happy Meal* (dir. Nick Atkins), *Tannos Collective* (Choreographer Stephen Tannos) and as part of *Club Cabaret* at Cake Wines in Redfern. Lewis also directed the short film *SKIN,* which has been nominated/screened in film festivals across Europe including London Shorts and Stockholm City Film Festival.

Cindy Cavero
Assistant Stage Manager

After graduating from the Academy of Film, Theatre and Television (AFTT) with a Diploma in Theatre Production, Cavero began working for Sydney Festival this year as her first step towards working in the arts industry, to sharpen her skills and gain more experience. She was fortunate to secure the roles of Assistant Stage Manager for *Set Piece,* directed by Nat Randall and Anna Breckon, performed at Carriageworks, and *Thaw* performed by Legs on the Wall, on the forecourt of the Sydney Opera House for the Sydney Festival season.

During her time with Sydney Festival, Cavero took on smaller general crew member roles and enjoyed the process of bringing a production to life on stage.

Anthea Doropoulos
Creative Producer

Anthea Doropoulos is an experienced dance producer and arts manager with 16 years' industry experience. As a creative producer she has fostered innovation in the dance sector by pioneering platforms for research, residencies, development, workshops and productions in inclusive and accessible dance practice for emerging and established dance artists.

In 2019 Doropoulos started her role as Creative Producer at Campbelltown Arts Centre and has successfully produced sell-out dance seasons *Explicit Contents, The Complication of Lyrebirds* and *Mirage*, presented in association with Sydney Festival. Doropoulos has developed a number of industry recognised programs including *Movement Movement* bringing the dance sector together annually to improve and grow dance connections in NSW and discuss the issues faced by the sector at large. Doropoulos has also overseen a number of projects that engage with emerging performance and dance artists.

Anthea Doropoulos has a strong passion for community engagement and works closely with a range of diverse artists and communities to support a more culturally rich arts community.

www.ingramcontent.com/pod-product-compliance
Lightning Source LLC
Chambersburg PA
CBHW050024090426
42734CB00021B/3411